Step 1
Go to www.openlightbox.com

Step 2
Enter this unique code
SRMWC5784

Step 3
Explore your interactive eBook!

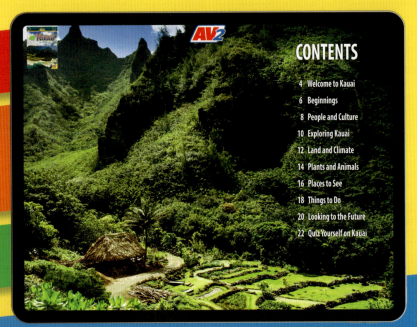

CONTENTS
- 4 Welcome to Kauai
- 6 Beginnings
- 8 People and Culture
- 10 Exploring Kauai
- 12 Land and Climate
- 14 Plants and Animals
- 16 Places to See
- 18 Things to Do
- 20 Looking to the Future
- 22 Quiz Yourself on Kauai

AV2 is optimized for use on any device

Your interactive eBook comes with...

Contents
Browse a live contents page to easily navigate through resources

Audio
Listen to sections of the book read aloud

Videos
Watch informative video clips

Weblinks
Gain additional information for research

Slideshows
View images and captions

Try This!
Complete activities and hands-on experiments

Key Words
Study vocabulary, and complete a matching word activity

Quizzes
Test your knowledge

Share
Share titles within your Learning Management System (LMS) or Library Circulation System

Citation
Create bibliographical references following APA, CMOS, and MLA styles

This title is part of our AV2 digital subscription

1-Year Grades K–5 Subscription
ISBN 978-1-7911-3320-7

Access hundreds of AV2 titles with our digital subscription.
Sign up for a FREE trial at www.openlightbox.com/trial

The digital components of this book are guaranteed to stay active for at least five years from the date of publication.

Kauai
"The Garden Isle"

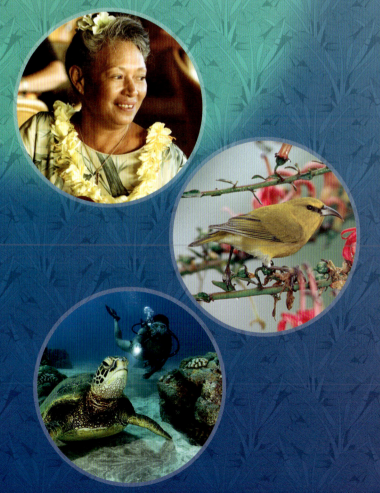

CONTENTS

- 2 Interactive eBook Code
- 4 Welcome to Kauai
- 6 Beginnings
- 8 People and Culture
- 10 Exploring Kauai
- 12 Land and Climate
- 14 Plants and Animals
- 16 Places to See
- 18 Things to Do
- 20 Looking to the Future
- 22 Quiz Yourself on Kauai
- 23 Key Words/Index

WELCOME TO Kauai

More than **60 movies** have been filmed on Kauai, including *Jurassic Park* and *Pirates of the Caribbean: On Stranger Tides*.

Kauai is home to the largest coffee farm in the United States. The Kauai Coffee Estate has more than **4 million coffee trees** on its land.

Only **10 percent** of Kauai can be reached by car, and only **70 percent** by foot.

Aloha! Welcome to Kauai! Kauai is an island in the U.S. state of Hawaii. This is the only state completely made up of islands. There are more than 130 islands in the **archipelago**. The Hawaiian Islands lie 2,397 miles (3,858 kilometers) east of San Francisco, California. People live on only seven of the islands. These are Hawaii, Maui, Molokai, Lanai, Oahu, Niihau, and Kauai.

Kauai is the northernmost Hawaiian Island. It sits about 72 miles (116 km) northwest of Oahu. Kauai is known as "The Garden Isle." This may be because it is often considered the greenest and most scenic of the Hawaiian Islands.

THE ISLAND OF Kauai

Population: 74,000 (2024)

Area: 552 square miles (1,430 sq. km)

Altitude: 5,243 feet (1,598 meters) at its highest point

County Seat: Lihue

Island Flower: Mokihana berry

Island Color: Purple

KAUAI—The Garden Isle

Beginnings

Kauai is the oldest of the major Hawaiian Islands. It formed about 5.1 million years ago, after millions of years of volcanic activity. The volcano that formed Kauai is no longer active. Its last eruption was about 400,000 years ago.

Captain Cook was on his third voyage to the Pacific when he came upon Kauai.

The first known people to settle on Kauai were the **Polynesians**. They arrived about 1,800 years ago from the Marquesas Islands, more than 2,000 miles (3,220 km) away. Captain James Cook, an English explorer, was the first European to set foot on Kauai, in 1778.

Over time, other people arrived from both Europe and the United States. Some set up businesses on the island. One of the first sugar **plantations** in Hawaii was formed on Kauai. Workers from many countries, including China, Japan, and the Philippines, arrived to work there. On August 21, 1959, Hawaii became the 50th U.S. state.

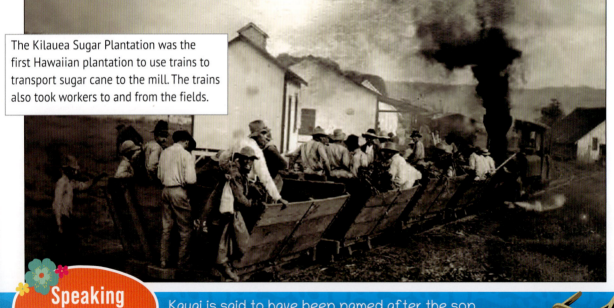

The Kilauea Sugar Plantation was the first Hawaiian plantation to use trains to transport sugar cane to the mill. The trains also took workers to and from the fields.

Speaking Hawaiian

Kauai is said to have been named after the son of Hawaii Loa, the Polynesian believed to have discovered the Hawaiian Islands. The word *Kauai* is pronounced "kuh-WAH-ee."

Kauai Timeline

200–400 AD
Polynesians settle on Kauai.

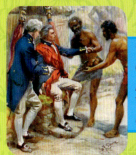

1778
Captain Cook lands his ships *Resolution* and *Discovery* at Waimea Bay, on the west coast of Kauai.

1820
Missionaries from New England arrive to convert Hawaiians to their religion.

1835
The first successful commercial sugar mill in all of Hawaii is established on Kauai.

1959
Hurricane Dot hits Kauai, resulting in $60 million worth of damage, mostly to the island's sugar cane crops.

1992
Hurricane Iniki devastates Kauai with wind speeds up to 160 miles (257 km) per hour.

2024
Kauai announces plans to build a coral nursery on the island to help improve the health of the island's surrounding coral **reefs.**

KAUAI—The Garden Isle

People and Culture

The Hawaiian people are **descendants** of the Polynesians who first inhabited the area. Much of Hawaii's culture and **traditions** date back to this time. Key elements of Hawaiian culture include traditional music and dance. Legends and other stories that explain island culture have been passed down from earlier generations.

Ancient Hawaiian music was also used as a form of storytelling. Elders taught children a combination of song and dance that relayed their people's past and **mythology**. *Mele*, or music, accompanies the traditional dance known as hula. Early instruments were made of hollowed-out gourds, stones, and bamboo sticks.

Every gesture or movement in hula dancing holds special meaning and helps relay the story being told.

Speaking Hawaiian

Ukulele, pronounced "OO-koo-LAY-lay," means "jumping flea." This may refer to the fast movement of a musician's fingers when playing the instrument.

Perhaps the best-known Hawaiian instrument is the ukulele, a small, stringed instrument brought to Hawaii by Portuguese settlers in 1879. King Kalakaua, Hawaii's ruler from 1874 to 1891, loved the ukulele so much that he incorporated it into traditional performances and songs. Today, the Kauai Ukulele Festival is held every year in April. Its purpose is to raise cultural awareness of the ukulele by showcasing both new and well-known artists.

Most ukuleles are made from the wood of the koa, a tree native to Hawaii.

Legend of Nunui
The Gentle Giant

Many features of Kauai's landscape are said to have been formed by mythical giants. Nunui was known as a gentle giant. He often made himself available to assist the locals. One day, he offered to help build a temple by gathering the huge stones needed for its walls.

When the wall was completed, the people of Kauai decided to thank Nunui by preparing a huge feast for him. After he ate, Nunui lay down to rest. He has yet to awaken and is now the mountain peak known as the Sleeping Giant.

KAUAI—The Garden Isle

Exploring Kauai

Kauai is the fourth-largest of the Hawaiian Islands. It is shaped like a circle. From its lush, mountainous center to the beaches covering almost half of its shoreline, Kauai has a variety of beautiful **landforms**.

Lihue
Lihue is Kauai's chief port and business center. It is located on the island's east-central coast. Key attractions in the town include a 1,000-year-old **aquaculture** reservoir and a historic sugar plantation.

Mount Waialeale
Mount Waialeale is a mountain mass in central Kauai. Its highest peak, Kawaikini, is the highest point on Kauai, with an elevation of 5,243 feet (1,598 m).

Napali Coast
The Napali Coast formed from wind and water **erosion** over millions of years. Stretching 17 miles (27 km) along Kauai's north shore, it features high cliffs, green valleys, waterfalls, and sea caves.

Waimea Canyon
Waimea Canyon is known as the "Grand Canyon of the Pacific." It is 14 miles (23 km) long and about 3,600 feet (1,100 m) deep at its deepest point. Views from the Waimea Canyon Lookout include crested **buttes**, rugged cliffs, and deep gorges.

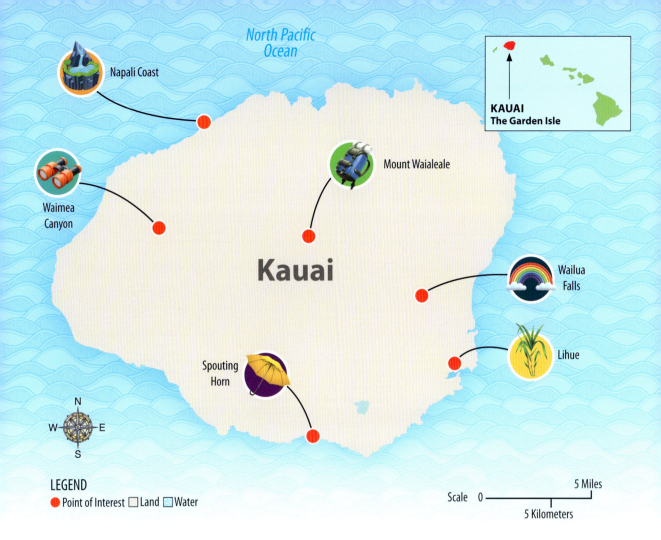

Wailua Falls
Wailua Falls is a dramatic two-streamed waterfall found near the end of the Wailua River. Its waters plunge for up to 173 feet (53 m), depending on rainfall. On sunny mornings, a rainbow may form as the sunlight meets the mist of the cascading waters.

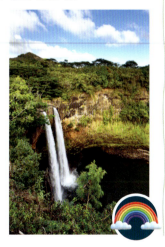

Spouting Horn
Spouting Horn is a spectacular blowhole on Kauai's south shore. As the surf hits the shore, the water flows into a **lava tube**. This force pushes a huge spout of water as high as 50 feet (15 m) into the air.

KAUAI—The Garden Isle

Land and Climate

Kauai is dominated by Mount Waialeale at its center. The mountain's slopes descend toward the coastline. The island features tall waterfalls, jagged cliffs, dense rainforests, swampy wetlands, and sandy beaches. Kauai is one of only five Hawaiian Islands to have rivers.

The island can be divided into four distinct geographic regions, each with its own features. The North Shore is the wettest of these regions and is known for its lush tropical greenery. The East Side has rich, flat land, making it ideal for growing coconuts and **taro**. The South Shore is known for its sunshine. Sand dunes can be found in some parts of this region, giving it a desert-like appearance. The West Side is the most rugged of the regions. Its mountainous terrain can make parts of this area difficult to navigate.

Polihale Beach, on Kauai's west coast, is one of Hawaii's longest beaches. It is about 17 miles (27 km) long and has dunes up to 100 feet (30.5 m) tall.

Speaking Hawaiian

The word *waialeale* means "rippling water." The mountain was likely named for its rainfall. *Waialeale* is pronounced "why-AH-lay-AH-lay."

Like the rest of Hawaii, Kauai has only two seasons. The dry season takes place between April and October, while the wet season is between October and March. Kauai has a **subtropical** climate, with warm temperatures and high humidity. Temperatures range from 65 to 85 degrees Fahrenheit (18 to 29 degrees Celsius). August is the island's hottest month. Kauai is home to one of the wettest spots in the world. Mount Waialeale averages 450 inches (11,430 millimeters) of rain annually.

Average High Temperatures

JAN	79°F (26°C)
FEB	78°F (25°C)
MAR	78°F (25°C)
APR	79°F (26°C)
MAY	81°F (27°C)
JUN	83°F (28°C)
JUL	84°F (29°C)
AUG	85°F (29°C)
SEP	85°F (29°C)
OCT	83°F (28°C)
NOV	81°F (27°C)
DEC	79°F (26°C)

Mount Waialeale's rainwater falls through crevices in the mountainsides. This makes it appear as if the mountain is weeping.

KAUAI—The Garden Isle

Plants and Animals

Kauai is home to a wide variety of plants and animals. It is well known for its beautiful flowers. An abundance of sea life is found in the oceans surrounding it. Several native bird species also make their home there.

Kauai Amakihi

This songbird lives only on the island of Kauai. While it could once be found across the island, the Kauai amakihi is now restricted to high-elevation forest areas. The estimated population is about 7,000. This is a significant drop from the year 2000, when the island had about 52,000 in residence.

Ohia Lehua

The ohia lehua tree is **endemic** to the Hawaiian Islands and is common on Kauai. It typically grows at low elevations, but has been found at heights above 4,000 feet (1,200 m) on the island. The tree has many uses. Besides providing a home for birds, it has leaves that can be used to make tea. Its wood is used to build houses and canoes.

Kamehameha Butterfly

The Kamehameha butterfly is endemic to several Hawaiian Islands, including Kauai. It is also the official insect for the state of Hawaii. Kamehameha butterflies are named after Hawaii's former royal family. They can often be seen around koa trees, as they are known to feed on sap.

Kauai Kokio

The Kauai kokio is a hibiscus that is endemic to Kauai and grows mainly on the island's northwest. It is typically found in forests at low elevations. Kauai kokio grows to a maximum of 33 feet (10 m) in height and has bright red blooms. It is considered one of the rarest plants in the world.

Yellow-Bellied Sea Snake

The yellow-bellied sea snake is the only sea snake known to swim in Hawaii's waters. These reptiles are found in coastal areas, living in waters less than 100 feet (30 m) deep. Yellow-bellied sea snakes can stay underwater for as long as three hours at a time. They grow to be 3 to 5 feet (1 to 1.5 m) long.

Hawaiian Monk Seal

The Hawaiian monk seal is the official state **mammal** of Hawaii and one of only two mammals native to the area. Adult seals are 5 to 7.5 feet (1.5 to 2.3 m) long and can weigh 400 to 600 pounds (181 to 272 kg). These **endangered** marine mammals are playful and curious. They can often be found on beaches after feeding.

Places to See

Visitors can enjoy the natural beauty of Kauai in a variety of ways. Napali Coast State Park is one of the island's top attractions because of its spectacular landscape. Helicopter tours are a popular way to experience the park. They provide guests with breathtaking views of the towering sea cliffs, waterfalls, and lush valleys in the region.

Boat tours are another way to experience the grandeur of the Napali Coast.

Kaneiolouma Heiau is an important cultural site on Kauai. Once an ancient Hawaiian village and place of worship, its remains give visitors insight into how Hawaiians lived in the past. **Hale** structures, fishponds, taro fields, and religious shrines dating back to the 1400s can all be seen at the site.

Four kii statues, each representing a Hawaiian god, stand near the road leading into the Kaneiolouma Heiau Hawaiian Village and Cultural Site.

The Kauai Hindu Monastery is tucked away in forests of the Wailua River valley. This active monastery is home to a small band of monks from many nations. Visitors are welcome to tour the outdoor grounds of the monastery, where they can view the site's many statues and temples. Guests can also make reservations to attend a time of worship in the main temple.

Statues of Hindu deities, such as Lord Shanmuga, are found throughout the grounds of the Kauai Hindu Monastery.

The entire Limahuli Garden and Preserve covers an area of 1,000 acres (405 ha).

Limahuli Garden and Preserve, on Kauai's North Shore, is in a **biodiverse** valley where visitors can explore 17 acres (7 hectares) of natural beauty and cultural history. Taro can be seen growing in lava terraces that date back several centuries. Gardens showcase the types of plants the Polynesians brought with them when they first came to the island.

The Kauai Hindu Monastery's Kadavul Temple is the **only all-granite, hand-carved Hindu temple** in the Western Hemisphere.

The Limahuli Gardens are home to almost **250** types of native plants and birds, **50** of which are almost extinct.

In 2023, Kauai's **1.42 million** visitors spent about **$2.76 billion**.

KAUAI—The Garden Isle

Things to Do

Hiking is a popular activity on Kauai. The island has some of the Hawaiian Islands' best hiking trails. The most renowned trail on Kauai is the Kalalau. It is 11 miles (18 km) long one way. Most hikers camp overnight and return the next day. Seeing green valleys, waterfalls, sea caves, and numerous other scenic vistas is what makes the Kalalau worth hiking.

Ziplining is a fun and exciting activity to do on Kauai. Riders can see stunning views of the island's jungles, mountains, and beaches as they zip through the air. Some ziplines are 2 miles (3 km) long, allowing for a variety of scenery all in one ride.

Kalalau Trail is considered a challenging hike, with limited areas of level ground.

Some people choose to explore Kauai on mountain bikes. The island offers trails suitable to various skill levels.

Kayaking the waters of the Wailua River is another way to experience Kauai. Kayakers can paddle past ancient villages and shrines on the river's calm waters. Some people leave their kayaks to take a short hike up to a waterfall known as Secret Falls. After swimming in the stream that leads to the waterfall, they hike back to their kayaks for the return trip.

The Wailua River is the only navigable river in the Hawaiian Islands, making it popular with kayakers.

Kauai has 50 miles (80 km) of white sand beaches, making it the perfect place for snorkeling. With just a mask, fins, and a snorkel, visitors can explore the underwater sights of Kauai. The island's coral reefs are home to a variety of marine life, ranging from tiny sea urchins to majestic Hawaiian green sea turtles.

Scuba diving allows visitors to Kauai the opportunity to spend an extended period underwater and meet a variety of sea creatures.

KAUAI—The Garden Isle

Looking to the Future

Tourism is an important industry on Kauai as it creates income for the people of the island. However, keeping up with the increased demands of tourism is creating **sustainability** issues for Kauai. When land is cleared to build more hotels and restaurants, animals and plants are forced out of their natural **habitat**. The island's human residents are often displaced as well. Tourism also creates pollution, whether through increased vehicle traffic or litter on beaches. This brings further harm to the land and its residents.

Today, local officials are working to find balance. One strategy has been to develop programs to educate visitors on the cultural and historical significance of the island. The goal of these programs is to encourage respect for the land. To reduce traffic pollution, shuttle buses now take people to various points on the island in large groups. Any new construction projects now undergo a review process to assess their environmental impact.

Signs are posted along Kauai's beaches to educate visitors on how to show respect for the island's natural environment.

Speaking Hawaiian

The Hawaiian word *pono*, pronounced "POH-no," means "to do what is right." People can honor this value by practicing sustainable tourism on Kauai.

Close to 73 percent of Kauai's sandy beaches are currently in some stage of erosion.

SPOTLIGHT on CHANGE

Ecotourism centers around awareness of the environment and the local community. The Sustainable Tourism Association of Hawaii works to provide environmentally responsible travel and education programs. Visitors to Kauai can help by choosing certified sustainable tours, supporting local businesses, and avoiding single-use plastics. Can you think of other ways to practice sustainable tourism?

Climate change is another issue facing Kauai. Sea levels are rising across the globe due to melting ice caps and glaciers. This is causing Kauai's beaches to gradually erode and its cliff faces to collapse. Vital habitats are being lost as a result. Rising sea levels contribute to **tsunamis**, hurricanes, and flooding. These events can wreak havoc on both the land and anything living on it.

Kauai is currently creating a climate adaptation plan to handle this issue. Its goal is to make sure the island is able to adapt to any changes that come. Areas of focus include how to improve the sustainability of the island's resources and protect its natural environment.

KAUAI—The Garden Isle

QUIZ YOURSELF ON Kauai

1. Which people first settled Kauai?
2. Why is Kauai known as the "Garden Isle"?
3. Which town is Kauai's chief port and business center?
4. How many seasons does Kauai have?
5. What is the best-known Hawaiian instrument?
6. What is Waimea Canyon also known as?
7. What is Hawaii's official state mammal?
8. When did Captain Cook land on the west coast of Kauai?

ANSWERS: 1. The Polynesian people **2.** It is considered the greenest and most scenic of the Hawaiian Islands. **3.** Lihue **4.** Two **5.** The ukulele **6.** The "Grand Canyon of the Pacific" **7.** Hawaiian monk seal **8.** 1778

HAWAII

Key Words

aquaculture: the farming of fish and seafood in fresh or salt water

archipelago: a group of islands

biodiverse: having a variety of life forms

buttes: isolated hills with steep sides and flat tops

climate change: long-term shifts in temperatures and weather patterns

descendants: people who are related to a person or group of people who lived in the past

endangered: in danger of no longer living on Earth

endemic: native to a particular place in the world

erosion: being gradually worn away by the action of water or wind

habitat: the place where an animal or plant naturally lives and grows

hale: traditional form of Hawaiian architecture

landforms: natural features of a land surface

lava tube: an underground passage formed by the flow of lava

mammal: a warm-blooded animal that has hair and feeds its young milk

missionaries: members of religious groups that are sent into an area to promote their faiths

mythology: a set of stories associated with a particular group or the history of an event

plantations: agricultural estates worked by laborers

Polynesians: people from a group of Pacific islands known as Polynesia

reefs: a ridge of material at or near the surface of the ocean

subtropical: relating to the regions bordering on the tropical zone

sustainability: the use of resources in such a way that they will continue to be available in the future

taro: a large-leaved plant grown for its edible starchy, rounded underground stem

traditions: information, beliefs, or customs handed down from one generation to another

tsunamis: long, high sea waves caused by earthquakes and volcanic eruptions

Index

animals 7, 14, 15, 17, 19, 20, 22

climate 12, 13, 21
climate change 21
Cook, Captain James 6, 7, 22

dance 8

hurricane 7, 21

Kalalau 18
Kaneiolouma Heiau 16
Kauai Hindu Monastery 17
Kawaikini 10

Lihue 5, 10, 11
Limahuli Garden and Preserve 17

Mount Waialeale 10, 11, 12, 13
music 8, 9

Napali Coast 10, 11, 16
Nunui 9

plantations 6, 10
plants 14, 15, 17, 20, 22
pollution 20
Polynesians 6, 7, 8, 17, 22

Spouting Horn 11

Wailua Falls 11
Wailua River 11, 17, 19
Waimea Canyon 10, 11

KAUAI—The Garden Isle

Get the best of both worlds.

AV2 bridges the gap between print and digital.

The expandable resources toolbar enables quick access to content including **videos**, **audio**, **activities**, **weblinks**, **slideshows**, **quizzes**, and **key words**.

Animated videos make static images come alive.

Resource icons on each page help readers to further **explore key concepts**.

Published by Lightbox Learning Inc.
276 5th Avenue
Suite 704 #917
New York, NY 10001
Website: www.openlightbox.com

Copyright ©2026 Lightbox Learning Inc.
All rights reserved. No part of this publication may be reproduced, stored in a retrieval system, or transmitted in any form or by any means, electronic, mechanical, photocopying, recording, or otherwise, without the prior written permission of the publisher.

Library of Congress Cataloging-in-Publication Data

Names: Letkeman, Candice, author.
Title: Kauai "the garden isle" / Candice Letkeman.
Description: New York : Lightbox Learning Inc., [2026] | Series: Hawaii | includes index. | Audience: Grades 2-3
Identifiers: LCCN 2024047326 (print) | LCCN 2024047327 (ebook) | ISBN 9798874506599 (library binding) |
  ISBN 9798874506605 (paperback) | ISBN 9798874507466 (ebook other) | ISBN 9798874506612 (ebook other)
Subjects: LCSH: Kauai (Hawaii)--Juvenile literature.
Classification: LCC DU628.K3 L48 2026 (print) | LCC DU628.K3 (ebook) | DDC 996.9/41--dc23/eng/20241114
LC record available at https://lccn.loc.gov/2024047326
LC ebook record available at https://lccn.loc.gov/2024047327

Printed in Guangzhou, China
1 2 3 4 5 6 7 8 9 0 28 27 26 25 24

122024
101124

Project Coordinator: Heather Kissock
Designer: Terry Paulhus

Photo Credits
Every reasonable effort has been made to trace ownership and to obtain permission to reprint copyright material. The publisher would be pleased to have any errors or omissions brought to its attention so that they may be corrected in subsequent printings. The publisher acknowledges Getty Images, Alamy, Minden Pictures, Shutterstock, and Wikimedia as its primary image suppliers. for this title.

View new titles and product videos at www.openlightbox.com